New Kid on the Block

By Tisha Hamilton

Marisa is moving with her family
to a new home in the city. As you
read, think about how Marisa feels
about her new neighborhood.

PEARSON

It was moving day. Marisa's father had a new job, so the family was leaving its old home. Their new **neighborhood** was in the city. Marisa loved her old neighborhood. There were bike paths and grassy lawns. There were backyards with swing sets.

Marisa stared out the car window. "Good-bye, old **neighborhood**!" she called. "I'll miss you."

"I'll miss our old neighborhood, too," her mother said. "I'm also excited about moving to the city." Marisa just shrugged.

 When they arrived at their new home, Marisa met a neighbor. Cara was eight, just like Marisa. She went to the same school that Marisa would go to. Best of all, Cara lived across the hall in the same apartment building.

⬤ "Come on, I'll show you around the
neighborhood!" Cara said. Marisa
wondered what there was to see. She knew
she would not see swing sets or grassy
lawns. She would not see a good place to
ride her bike.

Cara took Marisa to a park down the block. Marisa's father went with them. Marisa could hardly believe her eyes. There was a playground with swings and a slide. There was a bike trail. Best of all, there was a wide grassy lawn. It was perfect for turning **cartwheels**.

Marisa did a few fast **cartwheels** on the lawn. "You're good at cartwheels," Cara said.

"I can teach you how," Marisa said. They spent the afternoon practicing cartwheels. They had so much fun!

 Marisa was learning about her new neighborhood, but there were still things she missed. Marisa used to love going to Mrs. Green's bookstore near her old house. It was just like a **library**. Mrs. Green let her read any of the kids' books. Sometimes they shared a snack.

But then Cara took Marisa to the **library** on their block. There were big beanbag chairs to sit on. There were great books to read. Everyone was very friendly.

When Marisa's mom needed milk, Cara took them to a grocery store around the corner. The owner's name was Max. He gave the girls free pretzels. "Welcome to the neighborhood," he told Marisa's mother. Marisa was having so much fun that she forgot about missing her old neighborhood.

⬤ Marisa and Cara ate their pretzels. "I'm beginning to like it here," Marisa said. Cara smiled at Marisa. Marisa smiled back.

One night Marisa was not smiling. She was beginning to feel **nervous**. Tomorrow would be her first day at a new school. She didn't know anyone there.

"You know Cara," Marisa's mother said. "Why don't you go talk to her?" Marisa was already in her pajamas, but that didn't matter. She was only going across the hall.

"Don't be **nervous**," Cara told Marisa. "School will be so much fun. You'll meet all my friends." Marisa felt better about school.

Later, Marisa snuggled under the covers. "I never wore pajamas to visit a friend in my old neighborhood," she thought.

At school the next day, Marisa met all of Cara's friends. Amy and Marisa had the same backpack. Leo liked to read the same books as Marisa. Then Cara told everyone about Marisa's cartwheels.

"Teach me!" Marisa's new friends cried. Marisa couldn't wait for **recess**.

At **recess** Marisa taught everyone how to do cartwheels. It was the best day ever! Marisa loved her new neighborhood. Now she loved her new school, too.

Glossary

cartwheels sideways handsprings with the hands placed on the ground and the legs lifted over the head

library a place where books can be read and borrowed

neighborhood a small part of a city or town

nervous feeling fear or expecting trouble

recess a time to stop schoolwork for a little while, to play or relax